Contents

A musical timeline 4

Music begins 6

Music moves and changes 8

New ideas 10

A golden age 12

New directions 14

Recording history 16

Popular music 18

Mixing styles 20

Techno time 22

The power of music 24

The future of music 26

Key dates 28

Glossary 30

Find out more 31

Index 32

Historical time is divided into two major periods. BC is short for "before Christ" – that is, the time before the Christian religion began. This is the time up to the year 1 BC. AD is short for "Anno Domini". This is Latin for "in the year of our Lord", meaning the time from the year 1 BC to the present. For example, when a date is given as AD 1000, it is 1000 years after the year 1 BC. The abbreviation c. stands for *circa*, which is Latin for "around".

Any words appearing in the text in bold, **like this**, are explained in the glossary.

A musical timeline

Ever since people could use their voices to sing, or beat their hands to a **rhythm**, music has been an important part of our world. If you walk around a city today you will hear music playing in shops and cars. You might hear people humming or whistling, or see musicians playing in the streets.

All around us, people are listening to music through headphones.

This book looks back at how music has changed through history. All around the world, different people made and shared new instruments and sounds. People played music to celebrate festivals and during **religious ceremonies**. Singers also used music to express ideas about problems in the world. As new **technology** was invented, music was made and listened to in new and different ways.

The didgeridoo may have been played in Australia for over 40,000 years.

IC

ctronica

www.raintreepublishers.co.uk
Visit our website to find out
more information about
Raintree books.

To order:
☎ Phone 0845 6044371
🖹 Fax +44 (0) 1865 312263
🖳 Email myorders@raintreepublishers.co.uk

Customers from outside the UK please telephone +44 1865 312262

Raintree is an imprint of Capstone Global Library Limited,
a company incorporated in England and Wales having its
registered office at 7 Pilgrim Street, London, EC4V 6LB
– Registered company number: 6695582

Text © Capstone Global Library Limited
First published in hardback in 2011
Paperback edition first published in 2012
The moral rights of the proprietor have been asserted.

Edited by Louise Galpine and Diyan Leake
Designed by Richard Parker
Original illustrations © Capstone Global Library Ltd 2011
Illustrated by Jeff Edwards
Picture research by Hannah Taylor
Originated by Dot Gradations Ltd
Printed and bound in China by CTPS

ISBN 978 0 431 02557 5 (hardback)
14 13 12 11 10
10 9 8 7 6 5 4 3 2 1

ISBN 978 0 431 02565 0 (paperback)
15 14 13 12 11
10 9 8 7 6 5 4 3 2 1

British Library Cataloguing in Publication Data
Guillain, Charlotte – Music : from the voice to electronica.
– (Timeline history)
780.9-dc22
A full catalogue record for this book is available from the
British Library.

Acknowledgements
We would like to thank the following for permission to
reproduce photographs: akg-images pp. **10** top (Erich
Lessing), **13** top (North Wind Picture Archives), **14** top
(RIA Novosti), **18** (africanpictures); Alamy Images pp. **16**
(© Danita Delimont), **22** top (© PYMCA); Corbis pp. **6** (Joerg
Carstensen), **10** bottom (epa/Michael Reynolds), **13** bottom
(The Art Archive), **22** bottom (Roy Morsch), **25** bottom
(Reuters/Fred Prouser); Getty Images pp. **9** (Jason Childs),
12 (Hulton Archive), **15** (Time Life Pictures/Herbert Gehr),
17 top (Frank Driggs Collection), **19** top (Michael Ochs
Archives), **19** bottom (Redferns/David Farrell), **21** top (DAJ),
27 left (C. Brandon); Lebrecht p. **20** (David Farrell); Lebrecht
Music & Art Photo Library p. **8** bottom; Masterfile p. **26**;
Photolibrary pp. **4** top, **4** bottom (Dallas & John Heaton), **8** top
(Daniel Thierry), **11** (The British Library), **14** bottom (Antique
Reseach Centre), **27** right (Imagesource); Press Association
Images p. **7** bottom (AP); Rex Features pp. **21** bottom (Ian
Dickson), **23** (Sipa Press), **24** (Nils Jorgensen), **25** top;
© Romare Bearden Foundation/DACS, London/VAGA, New
York 2010 p. **17** bottom (Photo: Corbis/Christie's Images); The
Art Archive p. **7** top (Egyptian Museum Cairo/Dagli Orti).

Cover photograph of a media player reproduced with
permission of istockphoto (© Andrey Volodin).

We would like to thank Patrick Allen for his invaluable help
in the preparation of this book.

Every effort has been made to contact copyright holders
of material reproduced in this book. Any omissions will be
rectified in subsequent printings if notice is given to the
publisher.

Disclaimer
All the Internet addresses (URLs) given in this book were valid
at the time of going to press. However, due to the dynamic
nature of the Internet, some addresses may have changed, or
sites may have changed or ceased to exist since publication.
While the author and publisher regret any inconvenience this
may cause readers, no responsibility for any such changes can
be accepted by either the author or the publisher.

Timelines

The information in this book is on a timeline. A timeline shows you events from history in the order they happened. The big timeline in the middle of each page gives you details of a certain time in history (see below).

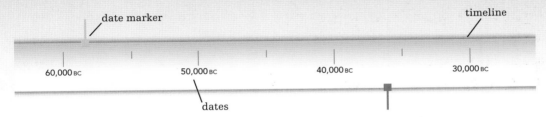

date marker

timeline

60,000 BC   50,000 BC   40,000 BC   30,000 BC

dates

Some dates are exact. For example, the first MP3 player was sold in 1998. Others are more general because early people did not keep written records, or the event may have happened over a period of time. The smaller timeline at the bottom of each page shows you how the page you are reading fits into history as a whole. You will read about music from all around the world. Each entry on the main timeline is in a different colour. This colour shows you which continent the information is about. The map below shows you how this colour coding works. Pale green indicates events that took place on more than one continent or worldwide.

North America

Europe

Asia

Africa

South America

Australia and Oceania

Worldwide

People first made music when they were able to use their voices and beat out a **rhythm**. Human beings have always made music. Early humans sang and made simple instruments from objects they found and from animals they killed. Paintings tell us that music was played at special festivals, in palaces, or for religious reasons.

c.58,000 BC

Neanderthals were an early type of human. Around this time, Neanderthals started making sounds with their voices. They had a special bone in their necks, called a hyoid bone, which meant they were able to sing and chant.

60,000 BC	50,000 BC	40,000 BC	30,000 BC

c.37,000 BC   EARLY HUMANS

Cro-Magnon people made flutes made from bone. They were some of the earliest modern humans living in Europe. Early modern humans had begun life in Africa thousands of years before. Over time, these people moved north and took over from Neanderthals and other early humans already living in Europe.

*c.*4,000 BC
Egyptians were playing music around this time. Over time, Egyptian instruments included tambourines, copper trumpets, lutes, oboes, and a stringed instrument like a harp, called a lyre.

20,000 BC   10,000 BC   1 BC

*c.*7,000–5,000 BC
People in China made flutes from the wingbones of birds. They are the earliest examples of musical instruments that can still be played.

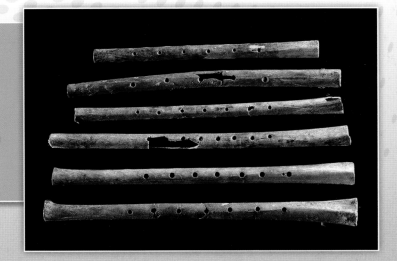

Music moves and changes

As people all around the world began to travel further, musical instruments were played in more places. People started to change and develop the way the instruments were used. There were new ways of playing music and performing.

c.600 BC

At this time, people in India were playing a stringed instrument called the bin. It was made of two **gourds** connected by a wooden body. This was one of the first hollow instruments and it was played by plucking the strings. The vina is a later version of bin which is still played today (right).

600 BC   400 BC   200 BC   1 BC   AD 200

c.300 BC

The Seikilos epitaph (left) is a Greek song. Once people started to write down musical notes, they could pass on music from place to place and through time.

AD 800   GAMELAN

People made stone carvings of gamelan instruments on the Borobudur Buddhist temple in central Java, Indonesia. Gamelan groups are still popular in Indonesia. Their name comes from a word meaning "to hammer". Gamelan orchestras play many **percussion instruments**, such as drums, xylophones, and gongs.

AD 400   AD 600   AD 800   AD 1000

AD 500

People in Peru were playing musical instruments such as flutes and drums. They probably played in groups for **religious ceremonies**.

AD 1000

Minstrels began travelling in Europe. They sang and played instruments to entertain, as well as performing dancing or juggling at fairs and festivals.

New ideas

During the 1200s to 1600s there were many firsts in the world of music. People discovered new inventions that changed the type of instruments that were made and how music was passed on. In many countries a **classical** style of music began that is still played and listened to today.

1200s

People began to develop instruments with keyboards. This picture from the **Middle Ages** shows an organ being pumped with bellows as well as a tuba (wind instrument), psaltery (plucked string instrument), fiddle, and bell-like cymbals.

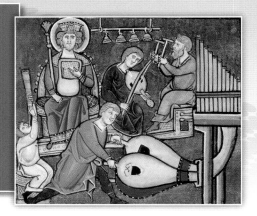

1200   1255   1310   1365   1420

1279 OPERA

During the Yuan **dynasty** (1279–1368), the golden age of Chinese classical **opera** began. Opera is a performance that tells a story through singing and musical instruments. Different types of opera are performed around the world. Some of the **traditions** and characters in Chinese classical opera, such as clowns, gods, and warriors, are still used today.

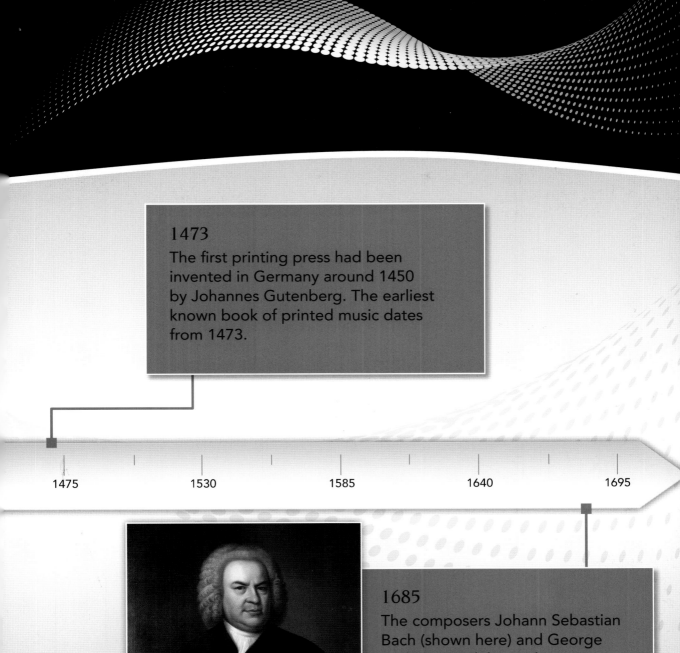

1473

The first printing press had been invented in Germany around 1450 by Johannes Gutenberg. The earliest known book of printed music dates from 1473.

1475   1530   1585   1640   1695

1685

The composers Johann Sebastian Bach (shown here) and George Frideric Handel were born in Germany. They wrote classical music in a style called **Baroque**.

A golden age

The period from the late 1600s through to the 1700s is known as the golden age of Western **classical** music. Two great classical composers, Mozart and Beethoven, were born and began to perform and compose in their childhood. The piano became the most important keyboard instrument and **opera** became very popular in Europe.

1698

Antonio Stradivari was making very high-quality violins in Italy. Some still exist today and are called Stradivarius violins.

1709 THE PIANO

The piano was invented in Italy. The proper name for a piano is *pianoforte*, which means "soft and loud" in Italian. It was the first keyboard instrument that a musician could choose to play loudly or softly.

| 1690 | 1700 | 1710 | 1720 | 1730 |

1756

The composer Wolfgang Amadeus Mozart was born in Salzburg, Austria. By the age of seven he was already famous. He wrote many famous pieces of church music as well as operas and music for orchestras.

1770s

African-American slaves in the United States sang rhythmic work and **spiritual songs**. These songs had started in West Africa. One singer would call out and the other singers would answer.

1740   1750   1760   1770

1770

The composer Ludwig van Beethoven was born in Bonn, Germany. He lost his hearing by 1819, but went on to write many famous pieces for piano and orchestra.

Western **classical** composers such as Chopin and Brahms, and the **opera** composers Verdi and Wagner, began to compose in a style known as **Romantic** music. Romantic composers wanted to use music to explore feelings and emotions. Other new musical styles started in the United States and inventors began to find ways to record music.

1840

The Romantic composer Pyotr Ilyich Tchaikovsky was born in Russia. He wrote music for orchestra, operas, and ballets such as *Swan Lake* and *The Nutcracker*.

1830   1840   1850   1860

1860

Pandit Vishnu Narayan Bhatkhande was born in India. He started the first music schools in India and helped more people to enjoy classical Hindustani music.

1877

Thomas Edison invented the **phonograph**. Now people could record and replay music for the first time.

1898

Paul Robeson was born in New Jersey, USA. He was an African-American **bass** singer and actor. He also spoke out about **civil rights** and peace.

1870   1880   1890   1900

1890 THE BLUES

Blues music was developing in the southern United States. "The blues" was started by African Americans. It came from **spiritual songs** and work songs and used musical **chords** in a special order. Blues singers often sang about lost love and how hard life was.

Recording history

People began to discover new ways of recording and playing back music. Flat records played on gramophones began to replace the cylinders used on Edison's **phonograph**. Meanwhile, many new styles of music became popular and travelled all over the world.

1906

The Canadian inventor Reginald Fessenden broadcast the first programme of voice and music on the radio in the United States. He played a recording of Handel's music and played a Christmas carol on the violin.

1914

Sir Apirana Ngata, a Maori **politician** in New Zealand, helped to make Maori songs popular. He helped to keep Maori musical **traditions**, such as the **haka**, alive.

| 1900 | 1902 | 1904 | 1906 | 1908 | 1910 |

1914

Tango music and dance spread from Argentina to Europe and the United States. Dancers held their partners close and moved in a dramatic way. The tango is still popular in Argentina as well as around the world.

1915

Jazz music was made popular in New Orleans, USA by groups such as the Original Dixieland Jazz Band (right). Jazz spread across the country by 1916 and the first jazz recordings were made in 1917.

| 1912 | 1914 | 1916 | 1918 | 1920 |

1920   THE HARLEM RENAISSANCE

A group of African-American writers, artists, and musicians was based in Harlem, New York, giving rise to the movement known as the Harlem Renaissance. Musicians such as Duke Ellington and Louis Armstrong made black American music popular across the world. This painting by Romare Bearden, a Harlem Renaissance artist, is called "Show Time".

Popular music

The development of electricity had a big impact on the world of music and recording. In the middle of the 1900s people started listening to recorded popular music. Ordinary people could now afford to buy new **vinyl** records to hear their favourite songs.

1920s

Highlife music became popular in West Africa. This dance music took sounds such as **jazz** from the United States and included many horns (saxophones and brass wind instruments) and guitars. Oscarmore Ofori (right, with guitar) was a popular highlife composer.

1920   1925   1930   1935   1940

1925

The Philadelphia Orchestra made the first electrical recording of music. They played music by the French composer Saint-Saëns.

1930s

Mariachi music started to become popular all over Mexico. Mariachi bands usually include violins, trumpets, and guitars. They were originally street musicians.

1935

Scientists demonstrated the first tape recorder in Germany.

1950

In the United States, the **blues** developed into **rock and roll**. By 1956 Elvis Presley (right) was an international star. Meanwhile, Ella Fitzgerald became famous for singing popular songs by great American songwriters.

1945　　　　1950　　　　1955　　　　1960

1956

The first Eurovision Song Contest was held in Switzerland.

1959　THE MOTOWN SOUND

The **record label** Tamla Motown Records started in Detroit, USA. Musicians such as Marvin Gaye, Stevie Wonder, and The Supremes (left) all recorded with Motown. It was the first record label owned by an African American, making records with a special soul sound.

Mixing styles

As popular music became a part of everyday life, musicians started to mix and experiment with styles. Many singers began to use music to talk about big issues such as war, poverty, and racism. Technology brought further changes to music, with new electric instruments and styles.

1960 MAKOSSA MUSIC

Makossa music started to become popular in West Africa. Makossa has a strong **bass rhythm**. Makossa musicians play horns and guitars with a picking sound. The first Makossa **percussion instruments** included bottles hit with sticks.

1963

Folk singers such as Bob Dylan and Joan Baez became famous singing songs to protest against war and injustice in the world.

1960　1961　1962　1963　1964　1965　1966

1962

The Beatles won fans all over the world. They started by copying **rock and roll** styles from the United States before writing many famous songs with their own sound.

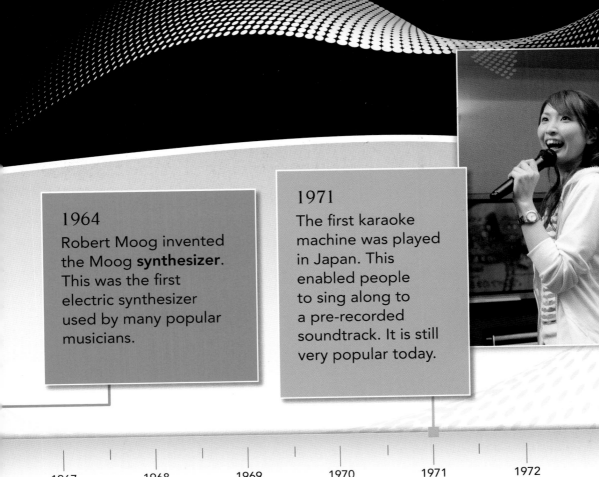

1964
Robert Moog invented the Moog **synthesizer**. This was the first electric synthesizer used by many popular musicians.

1971
The first karaoke machine was played in Japan. This enabled people to sing along to a pre-recorded soundtrack. It is still very popular today.

1967   1968   1969   1970   1971   1972

1970s
Bob Marley and the Wailers made rhythmic Jamaican reggae music popular all over the world. Reggae is often linked to the Rastafarian religion that is practiced in Jamaica.

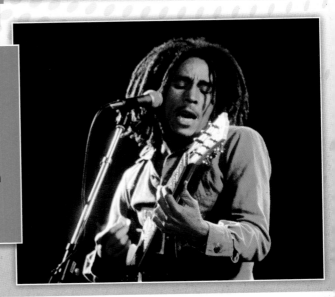

present day

Techno time

Towards the end of the 1900s, technology started to become more and more important to music. Technology affected the sound when music was played live and when it was recorded. People also started listening to music in new ways, using portable music players and watching music videos.

1974 HIP HOP HERC

Hip hop culture and music began in the Bronx, New York. DJ Kool Herc played the first hip hop music. People breakdanced in the streets to his music (right) and he started the idea of rapping by calling out as he played records. As well as music, hip hop culture includes graffiti writing and fashion.

1974   1975   1976   1977   1978   1979

1979

The Japanese company Sony invented the Walkman with its small headphones. For the first time people could walk around listening to music on cassettes.

1983

The MTV channel had been launched in 1981 and soon record companies were spending more and more money on music videos. In 1983 Michael Jackson's *Thriller* (left) cost $500,000 to film.

1980   1981   1982   1983   1984

1980s

Companies began manufacturing compact discs (CDs). The digital recording used on CDs gave music a better sound quality. CDs were also harder to break than **vinyl** records or cassettes.

1983

Musical Instrument Digital Interface (MIDI) was invented. This meant different electronic musical instruments could work together and that computers could be used to compose and record music.

The power of music

The Live Aid concerts that took place in 1985 showed how powerful popular music could be. The event raised around £150 million for **famine relief**. The power of music continued into the 21st century, with millions of people watching television shows such as *The X Factor*.

1985

The Live Aid concerts were held to raise money for starving people in Ethiopia. It was the biggest broadcast ever held. Musicians were talking about the problems in the world again.

| 1985 | 1987 | 1989 | 1991 | 1993 |

Late 1980s

Soukous dance music from central Africa spread to other parts of the continent and on to London and France.

1990s

Automated Harmonization of Melody in Real Time (AHMRT) was introduced. This technology can make a singer's voice sound in tune with the music.

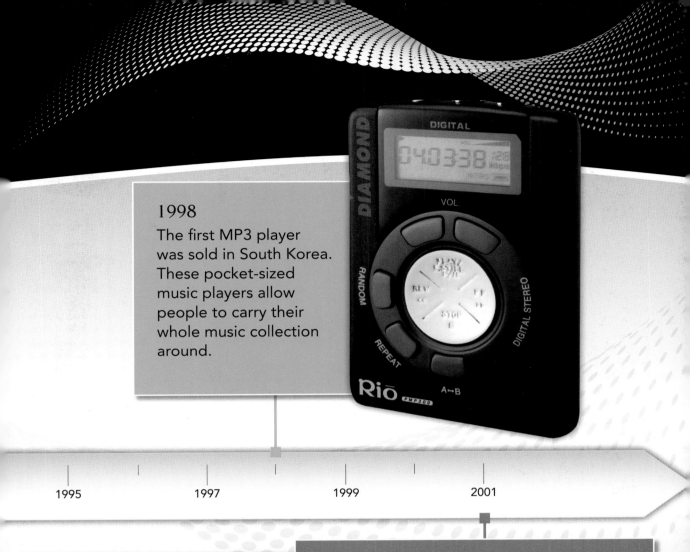

1998

The first MP3 player was sold in South Korea. These pocket-sized music players allow people to carry their whole music collection around.

1995   1997   1999   2001

2001   ANYONE CAN BE A POP STAR

The TV programme *Pop Idol* was made in the UK. *American Idol* followed in 2002 and was won by Kelly Clarkson (left, shown performing with Will Young, winner of the first *Pop Idol* series). Programmes such as these and *The X Factor* let people compete on television to win a deal with a **record label**. These programmes influence which types of music many people listen to.

The future of music

Music technology

All through history, **technology** has made a big difference to the music we play and listen to. When the printing press was invented, many more people than before could read and perform great music. Machines invented to record and play music, such as Edison's **phonograph**, let many more people hear all kinds of music. People using the Internet can find and listen to any song they want in seconds. They can also put their own music on the Internet for anyone to listen to.

| 2000 | 2002 | 2004 | 2006 | 2008 |

2000
Websites such as MySpace and YouTube mean that a musician or singer does not need to have a deal with a **record label** in order to be heard by people all over the world.

2004
Songs **downloaded** from the Internet were included for the first time on the UK and US music charts.

People have always travelled and spread musical styles and instruments around the world. Today, television and the Internet mean that we can listen to music from any country whenever we want.

People use music to share how they feel and say what they think about the world's problems. Music is played for **religious ceremonies** and celebrations. Nobody knows what sort of music people will play and listen to in the future or how they will make it. But people all over the world will probably always make music for the same reasons as musicians thousands of years ago.

Present ——————————————————————————— Future

Present

Digital recording software is now available for anyone to record all styles of music, using only a laptop computer.

Key dates

c.37,000 BC
Cro-Magnon people make flutes from animal bones.

c.7,000–5,000 BC
People in China make flutes from bird bones.

300 BC
In ancient Greece people start to write down musical notes.

AD 1200s
People begin to develop instruments with keyboards.

1685
The composers Johann Sebastian Bach and George Frideric Handel are born in Germany.

1709
The piano is invented in Italy.

1877
Thomas Edison invents the **phonograph**.

1890
Blues music is developing in the southern United States.

1906
The first programme of voice and music is broadcast on the radio in the United States.

1915
Jazz music is becoming popular in New Orleans, USA. By 1916 it has spread across the country and the first recordings are made in 1917.

1935
Scientists demonstrate the first tape recorder in Germany.

1950s
Rock and roll starts in the United States. By 1956 Elvis Presley is an international star.

1962
The Beatles win fans all over the world.

1974
Hip hop culture begins in the Bronx, New York.

1980
Companies begin manufacturing compact discs.

1985
The Live Aid concerts are held to raise money for starving people in Ethiopia.

1998
The first MP3 player is sold in South Korea.

Present
Digital recording software is now available for anyone to record all styles of music, using only a laptop computer.

Glossary

Baroque style of music that began in Europe in the 1600s. It is very ornate and rhythmic.

bass low-pitched sound

blues music started by African Americans in the southern United States at the end of the 1800s. The lyrics often describe life's hardships.

chord group of three or more notes played together

civil rights rights and freedoms of all individuals

classical serious artistic music

download transfer of files from a server to an individual computer

dynasty period of rule of a particular family

famine relief food aid sent to countries where many people are starving

folk style of traditional music, that used to be spread by word of mouth rather than written down

gourd dried shell of a hard-skinned fruit

haka traditional Maori group dance, with forceful movements, stamping feet, and rhythmic shouts

hip hop music and culture that includes rap, breakdance, and DJing

jazz style of music developed by African Americans where musicians often improvise and follow distinctive rhythms

Middle Ages period from around the 400s to the 1500s in Europe

opera performance that tells a story through singing and music

percussion instrument instrument that makes a sound by being hit or shaken

phonograph early type of record player

politician person who takes active part in politics – for example, a member of the government

record label company that records and sells musicians' work

religious ceremony event to express belief or faith that includes special customs and music

rhythm regular or recurrent pattern or beat

rock and roll type of popular music that started in the United States in the 1950s

Romantic style of art, literature, and music that focused on emotions and the imagination

spiritual song religious song of African-American origin

synthesizer electronic keyboard instrument that can imitate other instruments or produce new, different sounds

technology invention and use of tools and machines

tradition culture, customs, and beliefs that are passed down from one generation to the next

vinyl type of plastic used to make gramophone records

Find out more

Books

Learning Musical Instruments series (Heinemann Library, 2007)
Rock Music Library series (Capstone, 2004)
World of Music series (Heinemann Library, 2008)

Websites

Visit the National Geographic world music website to find out about many different styles of music from around the world.
worldmusic.nationalgeographic.com

Find out more about timelines and what was happening at different times in history.
www.worldtimelines.org.uk

Places to visit

See over 1000 instruments from the Western orchestral music traditions.
Bate Collection
Faculty of Music
St Aldate's
Oxford OX1 1DB
Tel. 01865 276139
www.bate.ox.ac.uk

Interact with 60 years of British music history from Trad Jazz to Dub Step.
The British Music Experience
The O2
Peninsula Square
London SE10 0DX
www.britishmusicexperience.com

Index

African-American music 13, 15, 17, 19
AHMRT technology 24
Australia 4

Bach, Johann Sebastian 11
ballet 14
Baroque music 11
Beatles 20
Beethoven, Ludwig van 13
Bhatkhande, Pandit Vishnu Narayan 14
bin 8
blues music 15, 19

CDs (compact discs) 23
China 7, 10
classical music 10, 11, 12, 14
Cro-Magnon people 6
cymbals 10

didgeridoo 4
drums 9

Egypt 7
Eurovision Song Contest 19

Fitzgerald, Ella 19
flutes 6, 7, 9
folk music 20

gamelan orchestras 9
gongs 9
guitars 18

Handel, George Frideric 11, 16

Harlem Renaissance 17
highlife music 18
hip hop 22

India 8, 14
Indonesia 9
Internet 26

jazz 17, 18

karaoke music 21
keyboards 10, 12

Live Aid Concerts 24
lutes 7
lyres 7

makossa music 20
Maori music 16
mariachi music 18
MIDI technology 23
minstrels 9
Motown 19
Mozart, Wolfgang Amadeus 12
MP3 players 25
music videos 23

Neanderthals 6

Ofori, Oscarmore 18
opera 10, 12, 14
organs 10

percussion instruments 9, 20
Peru 9
phonograph 14, 16, 26
pianos 12, 13

Pop Idol/American Idol 25
popular music 18–21
Presley, Elvis 19
printed music 11

recording music 14, 16, 18, 26, 27
reggae music 21
religious ceremonies 9
rhythm 4, 6, 20
Robeson, Paul 15
rock and roll 19, 20
Romantic music 14

singing 6
Sony Walkman 22
soukous music 24
spiritual songs 13, 15
Stradivari, Antonio 2
Supremes 19
synthesizers 21

tambourines 7
tango 16
tape recorders 18
Tchaikovsky, Pyotr Ilyich 14
technology 22–3, 24, 25, 26–7
timelines 5
trumpets 7, 18

vina 8
violins 12, 16, 18

X Factor 25
xylophones 9